Business Start Up Mastery

The Guide to Business Strategic Planning

By: Rafael Johnson

9781635010336

I0510799

PUBLISHERS NOTES

Disclaimer – Speedy Publishing LLC

This book was originally printed before 2014. This is an adapted reprint by Speedy Publishing LLC with newly updated content designed to help readers with much more accurate and timely information and data.

Speedy Publishing LLC

40 E Main Street, Newark, Delaware, 19711

Contact Us: 1-888-248-4521

Website: http://www.speedypublishing.co

REPRINTED Paperback Edition: ISBN: 9781635010336

Manufactured in the United States of America

DEDICATION

I dedicate this book to my family. I fully understand that my success is also the success of my family and that I wouldn't have all of this without them.

TABLE OF CONTENTS

Publishers Notes.. 2

Dedication 3

Chapter 1- Be On Top of Your New Business............................. 5

Chapter 2- How to Master Work/ Life Balance..........................10

Chapter 3- Me-Time Plays a Vital Role....................................15

Chapter 4- Keeping Old Customers and Making New Ones..........20

Chapter 5- A Great Business Needs A Great Leader....................29

Chapter 6- Business Leaders Take the Lead and Empower 36

Chapter 7- How to be A Great Business Leader.........................46

About The Author...51

CHAPTER 1- BE ON TOP OF YOUR NEW BUSINESS

Don't know how to beat your competitors? Then, you have to make the right move! Beating your competitors cannot be done in just a few clicks of your fingers. You have to apply the best marketing schemes and improve your business strategies.

Whether you are new to business or not, it is easy for you to achieve the peak of your success. For your guide, get all the info you need here! Make your business resolutions and focus on your goals now!

Achieving business success is not as easy as you think. Before reaching your goals, you have to focus on the things that you need to do and refrain from doing things that can affect your business operations.

To achieve one's goal, most business owners prefer to make their own resolution. If you are one of them, you should know how to create an ideal one. You also need to understand the real significance of business resolutions and how effective it is.

Business Resolution Meaning and Characteristics

A business resolution is a formal expression of a decision, action, opinion and transaction. Every year, businesspeople create their own business resolution to improve their operations. It is also one way of taking their business into the next level.

In making a business resolution, it takes time and effort. Your business resolution should be filled with ideal concepts. It is also best to ensure that you always follow your resolutions whatever it takes.

For your guide, here are the different characteristics of a business resolution that you shouldn't miss to consider:

• Specific - In making a business resolution, make sure that it is specific. Say for instance, you need to indicate that you have to reach a certain quota for your sales every month. As advised, don't make multiple resolutions all at once.

• Measurable - Depending on your goals, you have to make a resolution that is measurable. Therefore, it is best to describe how each result will be measured. If your resolutions are not measurable, it is hard for you to track your progress.

• Acceptable – Not all business resolutions are effective. Some business owners neglect to follow their own pledges. If you don't want to be like them, you have to ensure that your resolutions are easy to achieve. So, it is best to ask first yourself whether you have the tools, resources or skills needed to achieve your goals.

• Realistic – In making a business resolution, you have to be realistic. It means that you have to guarantee that you can reach your desired goals. Say for instance, if it is impossible for you to operate 24-hours a day, you don't have to change your business schedules.

• Time-frame - The best business resolution has its own deadlines and endings. Say for instance, you can set a weekly or monthly period goal. You also need to ensure that you are following your business plan to avoid any problem.

After knowing the different characteristics of business resolutions, you are certain that you can reach your goals. Like other business owner, it would be easy for you to improve your company operations. You can also easily meet the demands of your customers.

Following your business resolutions is quite a tricky task. Sometimes, you will be tempted to do short-cuts or refrain from doing your usual activities. But, if you are highly motivated and eager to reach your goals, you will do the accurate and specific ways.

Being Organized is Essential

Whether you are new to business or not, you shouldn't miss to underestimate the term "organized". Being organized is a foundation of being productive. When you say organized, it doesn't mean that you have to clean your office or other essential things. Being organized has a broad and extensive scope. The real organization is a mental state and describes on how you think.

If you want to be organized, you need to spend enough time dealing with your stuff and learn how you can approach your work more effectively. To know more about the mentality of being organized, you can read the following paragraphs.

Top 5 Tips on How to Be Organized

To become organized, you don't need to follow any complicated task. Instead of worrying on how to do this, here are the top things you need to do:

1. Understand that being organized is not just about trying to get more items sort out. It also doesn't mean that you can't tactically buy some stuff that will help you become more organized. To become organized, you need to start in improving your state of mind.

2. To become organized, you have to consider stuff according to its purpose. It means that you don't need to keep things that are useless. You also need to ensure that your stuff has its own value. Say for instance, you don't need to keep your tables around your office if you are not using it.

3. Another best way to become organized is to know your priorities. If not, you will never know what you really want. It is also impossible for you to reach your specific goals, both personal and business concerns.

4. To become organized, you have to figure out the real you. Most business owners don't know how to define themselves. Some of them are also afraid to admit who they really are. But, if you are willing to accept the real you, you can easily know what you need to do and what you really want to achieve.

5. To get organized, you need to get all the things that are valuable to you. So, make sure that you get rid of the things that are not important to you. Then, start organizing the valuable things that you have.

Sorting out your business stuff is easy to do. Once you became an organized person, you are doing what you really love and your actions reflect to your personality. So, if you don't want some distractions, it is best to get rid of unwanted stuff. You also need to separate your identity from the items that you own.

If you don't know where to start from, you can start making your resolution. Just make sure that you will follow your resolutions whatever it takes.

CHAPTER 2- HOW TO MASTER WORK/ LIFE BALANCE

Balancing work and family life is a challenging task. However, achieving its stability encourages the improvement of valuable skills. If you know how to balance work and family life, you can easily enhance stronger family relationship while improving your business operations.

To balance your work and family defines that you have to give an equal attention to both areas. Creating this balance does not often come naturally and it requires discipline and organization. When it comes to work and family concerns, not all business owners don't know how to balance them. In fact, some of them sacrifice family events to attend business meetings.

Steps on How to Balance Work and Family Life

Balancing work and family life promotes mental and physical health. It also enhances your ability to be organized. To give you some hints, here are the different steps on how to balance your work and family life:

Step 1: Make a Realistic Expectation – The most essential ways to balance your work and family life is to realize that you are just a human being. It means that you don't have the ability to do everything all at once. As advised, you have to prevent setting unrealistic expectation. If not, it will end up to disappointment. Say for instance, if you may not be able to attend the school activity of your daughter, you don't have to feel guilty.

Instead, make a realistic goal by adjusting your schedule.

Step 2: Make an Ideal Schedule – The easiest way to track your work and family activity is to make your own schedule. Therefore, you have to write down all the things that you need to do. You also need to pick a huge calendar or poster board to track your commitments and special events.

Step 3: Prioritize Your Family – Whether you are too busy or not, you have to prioritize your family. However, it doesn't mean that you will spend most of your time with them. Depending on your choice, you can set a schedule when to hang out with them without sacrificing your business commitments. As advised, you can watch a movie together or play an outdoor game during your free time.

Step 4: Learn When to Say "No" – If you have a busy schedule, you should not allow other people to distract you. You have to follow your schedule. You also need to say no to go to work events if it means giving up too much time away from your beloved family.

Step 5: Leave Your Work at the Office and Focus on Your Family While at Home – As much as possible; don't bring your work at home. If you did, you will never spend a quality time with your family.

Instead of worrying at home, take time to bring the whole family to mall or other entertaining centers. You can also make creative ways for your children.

By following these multiple steps, you are confident that you can easily balance your work and family life. Therefore, you will never sacrifice anything to have a perfect and wonderful life. Just make sure that you know your priorities in life.

Self-Reward Principle

Achieving goals takes time and effort. Whether you have a short or long- term goal, you have to ensure that you are doing the best move to reach it.

Once you achieved your goals, it is best to reward yourself. Rewarding yourself is a cool and easy way to keep you motivated. These rewards are something meaningful to you. They should be something you are willing to work for.

The reward system can be done in various ways. Like others, you have to pick a reward you desire after reaching your goal. Then, once you reached your goal, you need to reward yourself as soon as possible.

Rewards come in various types. Depending on your choice, it can be a simple or elegant reward.

Importance of Rewarding Yourself for Reaching Goals

Why most people reward themselves for achieving their goals? If you don't know the reasons why, here they are:

• Rewards contour Your Behavior – Using rewards will turn your goals into habits. These rewards are also effective in maintaining a positive attitude. Rewards also make your daily transition into a healthy lifestyle. Therefore, rewards can help in developing your behavior and mental abilities.

• Great Tool for Motivation – Rewards allow you to stay on track. Whether you reward yourself a simple or grand stuff, it can help in encouraging you to continue succeeding. These rewards also give you something to work for. Then, once you achieved your goals, you will feel more contented and accomplished.

• Promotes Self-Confidence – Some people may underestimate your skills and potentials. If you continue to strive and achieve your goals, it can help in building your confidence. You can proudly say that you finally reach your goals. With rewards, you will feel good and allows you to celebrate your own success.

Rewards are something meaningful to you. They should be something you are willing to work for. To reach your goal, you should not use a reward that goes against what you are trying to accomplish. Say for instance, if your goal is to improve your productivity, never reward yourself with something that would interfere with your daily routine.

The best rewards should reflect the importance and size of your goal. Then, you also need to use rewards if they mean something you personally.

Say for instance, if you are not a big fan of English novel, never purchase a book as a reward. In addition, you should refrain from giving too much reward.

If you did, you will never focus on your goals, but to the reward itself.

As you can see, achieving any goal gives you a great and satisfactory feeling. Therefore, you should be excited about each milestone you reach. In some cases, the next step towards your goal seems even more challenging.

But, when you think about the reward and longing to have it, this will motivate you to make a right move. So, start practicing the reward system and expect that you will get your ultimate goals in life.

Chapter 3- Me-Time Plays a Vital Role

Even if you are too busy with your work and family life, you have to take time for yourself. If not, you will be burned out. Too much work is not advised. That's the reason why you have to divide your time for work, family and for yourself.

For most business owners, they don't need to focus on themselves. Instead, they prefer to make miracles on how to reach their goals in life. Now, you can also do the same thing without pressuring yourself. If you keep on working and neglect to prioritize yourself, you will feel weak.

Giving yourself a time plays a vital role for your success. Some people enjoy a cool bath while others prefer to take a walk in a park. Whatever activity you want to do, you have to do it right away. Just make sure that you have to make plans.

Tips on How to Take Time for Yourself

To take time for yourself, you don't need to follow any complicated step. At first, you need to look at your calendar. Then, determine the best time for yourself. Before deciding, make sure that you finished your commitments to both work and family members.

After knowing your schedule, you have to save that day. It means that you need to block out a time where you can fit in a little rest and relaxation.

Then, you have to know what you want to do. Depending on your choice, you can join an exercise class or any activity. You can also watch some events in your local area.

To relieve your stress at work, you have to nourish your mind and soul. You can do this through meditation, listening to relaxing or slow music, and filing your minds with visions of youth.

You can also breathe the fresh air, enjoy the sunshine or walk quietly in the woods. Though it is hard to do, you need to leave your problems behind for a little while.

Since you are taking time for yourself, it is best to be more relaxed while doing your preferred activity. In addition, you also need to nurture your body. To do this, you can get a massage to renew and rejuvenate body.

Depending on your choice, you can also make a healthy meal or take a relaxing bath.

Why do you need to take time for yourself? Taking time for yourself provides multiple benefits and here they are:

• Self-Reflection - This can help in developing your personal growth. This allows you to become aware of your experiences. If you reflect upon your life, you are also getting the wisdom to move forward. With self-reflection, you can decide what you want to do and what you don't want.

• Unplug from Society - Each day, people are surrounded by media. Some use social networking sites and televisions to get information. Through taking time to yourself, you will never attach to these different forms of media. It means that you will plug into your own thoughts, feelings and emotions.

• Self Influence – This is essential in your personal growth and development. Unlike others, you don't have to live your life influenced by the media. If you have time for yourself, you will know what you really want without considering the different desires of other people.

With great benefits of taking time for yourself, you have to make the right move. Start adjusting your schedule and witness how it changes your life.

Keeping Up With Your Self Discipline Training

Creating a business resolution is quite fast and easy. The main tricky is its actual implementation. If you want to maintain your business resolution, regular practice is advised. However, how can you do the training if you are quite busy?

Though you are too busy, you can still change for the better. You can achieve your goals through showing that you are eager to reach it. With regular practice of your business resolution, you will soon realize that you are doing it naturally.

However, not all businessmen understand the significance of training. Some of them decide to skip their training, especially when they have an urgent meeting or event. Whether you have lots of things to do, you can still practice your business resolution. You just need to adjust your schedule and know your priorities.

To maintain your business resolution, you need to practice it every day. For your guide, here are some methods you can do to ensure that you are doing the right and effective way:

• Make Your Own Schedule – Once you already knew what you really want to do, you have to create an effective and attainable schedule. Simply jot down what you need to do every day and make sure that you follow it accurately.

• Don't Make Excuses – To become a successful business owner, you have to focus on your goal. If you already made your own resolution, you have no choice but to follow it.

Though you are busy with your work or family life, you have to set things right. You have to guarantee that you will practice your resolution no matter what it takes.

• Don't Make Shortcuts – Businesspeople make resolutions to improve their daily operations. They are also doing this to ensure that their business is getting better compared to the previous years. If you want to become a successful businessman, don't forget that there is no shortcut way of success. Therefore, you have to start at the bottom up to the peak of your success.

Training plays a vital role to reach your desired goals. At first, you may say that you will do the training because you are following your resolutions.

But, as time passes by, you will do the training like an ordinary activity.

So, instead of worrying about your business, start making a resolution and follow it accurately. Then, expect that you will get the fruitful result of your hard work.

CHAPTER 4- KEEPING OLD CUSTOMERS AND MAKING NEW ONES

Business networking is an effective method for finding new customers and forging new business relationships. Contacts with different groups or clusters would help you in getting greener opportunities.

For most businessmen, the more diverse their network is, the better it would be. Once you attend group meetings, you have the chance to get the business cards of other business tycoons. As a result, that would bring a great business development.

Benefits of Networking in Business – What Are They?

Networking provides multiple benefits to business. This can help in expanding your contact list and improving your sales base. It can also bring you in touch with various requirements to diversify your company.

Unlike other business owners, you should always network. It is essential to make a lasting first impression on various people that you will meet.

This impression you created will bring the better and wider business opportunities. Just make sure that you always keep in touch with the contacts you have gathered. In addition, you also need to help people in your network. With this, you can easily bring not just goodwill but business improvement as well.

In networking your business, you should also consider on how to improve it. You need some insights about networking and relationship to guarantee business success.

Networking helps the growth of your company. It is also effective in creating new products and expanding your ideas about the field.

Aside from the above mentioned, networking also helps in increasing your profits to a considerable degree. It also gives you the scope to get referrals and helps you to attain your targets in a fast and easy way.

Networking also provides a healthy relationship and a mutually beneficial rapport with your competitors, compatriots, clients and suppliers.

If you want a successful business, you have to do the networking strategy. Through this, you will enjoy a steady rise in your balance.

The Positive Mind Attitude

To overcome the different challenges of your life, you have to think positively. Instead of worrying about your flaws and insecurities, you need to face them. You have to keep on practicing the "I Can Do It" mentality.

The "I Can Do It" mentality plays vital role in your life. Whether you are facing simple or complicated challenges, you are certain that you can overcome it. You just need to believe in yourself that you can do it.

This "I Can Do It" mentality means that you have to eliminate all your negative thoughts. Though some people keep on saying that you can't do it, use it as a challenge. Never underestimate yourself because everyone has the power to reach an ultimate success.

If you are practicing this kind of mentality, it means that you need to eliminate excuses. So, don't let excuses get in the way of your goals. You have to focus on your dreams and achieve them through your positive thinking.

However, some people claimed that it is impossible for them to achieve success. Even if you commit mistakes and failed several times, it doesn't mean that you will never be successful.

Don't look at a failure at something negative. These flaws and failures can be used as your strength and way to do things better. Just don't let failure hold you back.

How Achieve "I Can Do It" Mentality?

Most people claimed this common phrase – "It is easier said than done". This statement is extremely true. Even if you want to think positively, there is always a time that you will think negative thoughts. The main question is how can you avoid negative thoughts and start practicing the "I Can Do It" mentality?

There is no complicated step in achieving the right mentality. At first, you need to focus on long-term goals.

You also need to remind yourself of your blessings and strengths. As advised, don't allow yourself to get into a spiral of negative thinking. When your negative thoughts arise, make destructions and start thinking with positive ones.

In addition, you also need to maintain a good relationship with others who have a positive mentality. This allows you to become more optimistic. You can also write down evidence of opportunities and positive activities every day. You can do this through making a journal.

Positive Affirmation and Your Business Goal

Positive affirmations are often used to impress the subconscious with a thought that can motivate and remind you about your talents. It also provides the confidence you need to reach your goals, business resolutions and other missions.

With regular use of positive affirmation, you can easily change your attitude, habits and behaviors. You can also use it to heal and find prosperity and romance.

How Affirmations Work?

Negative thoughts can be altered by using positive affirmations. If you don't know how to do it, you can use the following guides:

1. Decide What You Really Want - You just need to think about your life and the things that you want to have. Say for instance, if you want more money, use this as affirmation. Just be clear about your goal and do everything to achieve it.

2. Use the Present Tense when Making Affirmations – Most people make affirmations like "I will be a successful business". This statement claims that you will soon to be a successful businessman. To encourage you in reaching your goals, you have to say that "I am a successful businessman".

3. Always Be in Positive Mode – Whether you are speaking or writing your affirmations, don't forget to use positive phrases. Say for instance, if you want to get a high monthly sale, you need to say that "I Can Do It".

4. Always Remember Your Affirmations – To get what you really want, you have to repeat your affirmations several times. You also need to believe in yourself that you can easily do it. Then, you will realize that you are one step closer to your goal.

5. Be Persistent – Affirmations only work if you used them regularly. The more frequently you repeat your affirmations, the longer you say them. As a result, the quicker you will achieve your ultimate goal.

To make your affirmations stronger, you need to make them bold, clear and positive. When you start doubting your affirmations, don't forget to realize that your non-conscious brain is transmitting you a signal based on your conditioning. Above all, you have to keep recommitting to the process to get a successful result.

Take note that affirmations take some time. However, once you start its actual process, you will be surprised with its quick results.

At first, you will feel like you are spending too much time and effort. But, as time passes by, you will realize that the process begins to take over. So, all you need is to understand how to use your conscious faculties to strike into the phenomenal power of your non-conscious brains.

Business and Personal Resolution

If you are trying to excel professionally, you shouldn't miss to make a business resolution. Just make sure that you know what you really want and the exact things that you need to do to achieve it. With a successful business resolution, you can change your life in an instant. What are the benefits of making a business resolution?

The following will give you enough hints about the different benefits of business resolution:

Motivation

Making a business resolution is an effective way of boosting your level of motivation. This provides a sense of urgency to the work that needs to be accomplished. With this, you will be tempted to work in a fast and effective way. You will also not distracted with flaws and other related changes while reaching your goals.

Providing a Direction

Most people often find themselves wanting to change something in their lives. However, most of them don't know how to achieve it. With business resolution, they have a guide on how to do it. They just need to indicate what they want to achieve. They also need to know the different things they need to do to reach their goals.

Increased Success Rate

With accurate business resolution, you have a chance to improve your daily operation. As a result, you can easily know what are the things you need to do and the things that you need to avoid. Your resolution can be used as a tool to remind you that you can reach your goals. You just need to spend enough time and effort. Then, you will soon witness the prolific result of your hard slog.

Enhances Your Attitude

If you have a business resolution, you can easily control yourself. You will know your priorities and know how to handle your situation. Say for instance, if you keep on practicing your resolutions, you will soon realize that your daily routine is not the usual one. If you are not productive before, this resolution is an excellent guide to improve your work.

Get Organized

With the use of your business resolution, you will get organized. It means that you can manage your stuff and handles everything you need to do. You will also know how to balance your work and family life. If you are organized, chances to achieve your goals are extremely possible.

Limiting Stress

Your business resolution helps you in reducing stress. Without this guide, you may develop a tendency to jump from one project to another.

Then, you may realize that your overall production is a mess. So, instead of worrying about your hectic schedule and tons of unfinished projects, try to make a business resolution and follow it professionally.

Stay on Track

Your business resolution is a roadmap to help you get where you are going. You just need to play out a plan to keep you headed in the right direction. To do this, you need to lists the steps you need to take and you will get what you really want.

Increased Self-Confidence

With your business resolution, you will do the right and best way to achieve your goals. Once you achieve it, more and more people will continue to praise you. You will also feel a great satisfaction and fulfillment due to your hard work.

With various benefits of creating a business resolution, most businessmen desire to have one. If you are one of them, you should make sure that you are following your resolution. If not, you will never get its full benefits.

Maintaining your business resolutions is not as easy as you think. But, if you know what you need to do and eager to reach your goals, everything will turn out great.

The success of your business resolutions relies on your hands. So, whether you have a simple or complicated resolution, don't worry about it.

Try to focus on your goals. You also need to be ready and face the challenges while on process of achieving your goals.

Though it is hard to achieve, you need to focus on your goals. The main reason why you are making a business resolution is that you want to be better. To be better, you need to exert enough time and effort. Your success can never be achieved within a single wink of an eye. You have to earn it.

So, make a right move and see how your business resolution works.

CHAPTER 5- A GREAT BUSINESS NEEDS A GREAT LEADER

Napoleon once said: "One bad general does better than two good ones." It takes a moment for the sense of this to register, but it is the same as our modern saying that "too many cooks spoil the broth".

Having one set of instructions, even if they are flawed, is preferable to having two sets of perfect directions that, when enacted together without reference to each other, cause havoc.

This is the principle of leadership in a nutshell. It is all about maintaining focus and creating positive outcomes.

The same can be applied to individuals who strive to become leaders. There needs to be focus and determination. Advice can be given, but does not have to be heeded. History is full of leaders whose beginnings were disastrous, and had they listened to the naysayers of this world, the world would be a poorer place today.

Leadership can be learned. Some people are certainly born with leadership skills, but this is not a prerequisite for becoming a leader.

More important is dedication to the art of leadership. Leadership involves understanding how to inspire, influence and control how people behave. It is not a simple matter of shouting, or having a deep and booming voice; or being great in physical stature; Gandhi possessed none of these attributes, but managed to lead a nation and inspire millions around the world.

Sometimes, leadership may be no more than having a poignant message for a receptive audience at an opportune moment. Of itself, leadership is neither good nor bad; the world has known more than its fair share of evil and charismatic dictators.

In the world of business, the perception of leadership has changed from its early days when it largely mirrored the military model of leadership from the top down, with powerful individuals dominating large groups of less powerful people.

Nowadays, leadership in business is far more knowledge-driven. The lowliest employee may end up effectively leading the direction of a vast corporation through his or her innovative ideas. Anyone with critical knowledge can show leadership.

This is known as thought-leadership. In other situations, leadership can be about taking a stand for what you believe in, and trying to convince people to think and act differently.

Leadership has been variously described as the "process of social influence in which one person can enlist the aid and support of others in the accomplishment of a common task"; "creating a way for people to contribute to making something extraordinary happen"; "the ability to successfully integrate and maximize available resources within the internal and external environment for the attainment of organizational or societal goals"; and "the capacity of leaders to listen and observe, to use their expertise as a starting point to encourage dialogue between all levels of decision-making, to establish processes and transparency in decision-making, to articulate their own values and visions clearly but not impose them. Leadership is about setting and not just reacting to agendas, identifying problems, and initiating change that makes for substantive improvement rather than managing change".

There is truth to all of the above definitions, but they all apply to the ideals of leadership. So what of leadership gone awry?

Understanding the Dark Side

The dark side of any individual when allowed to go unchecked can create a rigid and dysfunctional personality that stifles creativity, and taints or ruins relationships.

When such characteristics are given reign in a leader, a self-righteous and bombastic person can result, who alienates the very people they are meant to inspire.

Compulsive leaders feel like they have to do everything themselves. They try to manage every aspect of their business, often refusing to delegate, and cannot resist having their say on everything. As they lack trust in others, they cannot let anyone else take responsibility, therefore they restrict personal growth in their team.

Compulsive leaders have many other traits. They are perfectionists who must follow highly rigid and systematized daily routines, and are concerned with status.

Thus they   strive to impress their superiors with their diligence and efficiency and continually look for reassurance and approval. This can lead to them becoming workaholics, and their team is viewed as failing if they don't keep pace. Spontaneity is not encouraged as this bucks the routine.

Despite this appearance of total control, such leaders can be fit to explode on the inside, and this can be the result of a childhood environment where unrealistic expectations were placed on them. Their attempts to keep control are linked to their attempts to suppress anger and resentment, which makes them susceptible to outbursts of temper if they perceive they are losing their grip.

Narcissistic leaders are focused on themselves. Life and the world revolve around them, and they must be at the center of all that is happening. Whilst they exaggerate their own merits, they will try to ignore the merits of others, or seek to devalue them, because other people's accomplishments are seen as a threat to their own standing.

The worst type of narcissistic leader cannot tolerate even a hint of criticism and disagreement, and avoid their self-delusions and fantasies being undermined by surrounding themselves with sycophants.

Where possible, they will attempt to use the merits of others for their own advancement, and think nothing of stepping on people to get ahead.

Their own feeling of self-importance means they are unable to empathize with those in their team, because they cannot feel any connection. Their only focus is on receiving plaudits that further bolster their sense of greatness. Such an attitude is often the result of a deep-seated inferiority complex, and thus no matter how much they are achieving; they will never feel it is enough.

Some narcissistic leaders take on a sidekick, but this person is expected to toe the line at all times, and serves only to reflect glory onto them and loudly approve of all that they do. Clever sidekicks can subtly manipulate the leader into focusing on the operational outcome of their plans, rather than just their own self-aggrandizement.

Ultimately, this type of leader can be very successful if their vision is strong and they get the organization to identify with them and think like they do. Such productive narcissists have more perspective, and can step back and even laugh at their own irrational needs.

Paranoid leaders are exactly as they sound: paranoid that other people are better than they are, and thus they view even the mildest criticism as devastating. They are liable to overreact if they sense they are being attacked, especially in front of other people. This can manifest itself in open hostility.

This attitude is the result of an inferiority complex that perceives even the most constructive criticism in the wrong way. The paranoid leader will be guarded in their dealings with other people because they do not want to reveal too much of themselves in case they display their weaknesses and are attacked or undermined. They may be scared that their position is undeserved, therefore can be deeply suspicious of colleagues who may steal their limelight or perhaps challenge for their position.

This is not always a wholly negative trait, however. A healthy dose of paranoia can be key to success in business, because it helps keep leaders on their toes, always aware of opportunities not to be missed. It is the opposite end of the spectrum to being complacent, and can make for a very successful venture.

Co-dependent leaders do not enjoy taking the lead, and instead seek to copy what others have done or are doing. They avoid confrontation and would rather cover up problems than face them head-on. Planning ahead is not their forte. They tend instead to react to whatever comes their way, rather than acting to alter outcomes or achieve goals.

Codependent leaders, therefore, are not leaders at all. They are reactionary and have the habit of keeping important information to themselves because they are not prepared to act upon it. This can clearly lead to poor outcomes because all the pertinent facts are not known to those below the leader who may be charged with making decisions.

This type of leader avoids confrontation and is thus liable to accept a greater workload for themselves rather than respond negatively to any request. They are also prone to accepting the blame for situations they have not caused.

Passive-aggressive leaders feel like they need to control everything, and when they can't they cause problems for those who are in control. However, they are sneaky in their ploys, and are very difficult to catch out. Their main characteristics are that they can be stubborn, purposely forgetful, intentionally inefficient, complaining (behind closed doors), and they parry demands put on them through procrastination.

Typically, if they feel they are not firmly in the driving seat, they will jump out and puncture the tires when no one is looking, then feign horror and pretend to search around for a tire iron.

This type of leader has two speeds: full speed ahead and stopped. When situations do not go their way, they will offer their full support for whatever has been decided, then gossip and back stab, willfully cause delays, and generally create upset. When confronted, they claim to have been misinterpreted. Passive aggressive leader are often chronically late for appointments, using any excuse to dominate and regain some control of the situation.

Dealing with passive-aggressive leaders is thus a draining and frustrating affair that saps energy. They are not averse to short outbursts of sadness or anger to regain some control, but are ultimately fearful of success since it leads to higher expectations.

CHAPTER 6- BUSINESS LEADERS TAKE THE LEAD AND EMPOWER

Leading people has nothing to do with managing them. Too many managers are trying to micro-manage their staff, all the while forgetting to lead them effectively.

If you want to become a strong leader you need to lead by example. This means you have to show your team that you are perfectly capable to set examples. By doing so, you will earn their respect and create lifelong devotees who would move mountains to please you.

A manager that only sits on his office and hide from his/her subordinate can't the respect that they need.

Ultimately the success of any business venture lies in the hands of its employees and NOT the managers. A manager's responsibility is to organize and manage business systems, systems that will see to the successful finalization of projects.

If your staff is unhappy it will soon show in their lack of productivity. This will influence your bottom line. Chances are customer complaints will start to amass and office gossip will run hot. This is counterproductive to running a well oiled machine – your business.

No organization can function for very long without the co-operation of its employees. Unfortunately, the necessity in any organization is that there are various levels of status within the team, and this can lead to conflicts if not managed properly.

The effective leader has to realize that the team under them is there because they have to be. Most employees work to earn money, not because they enjoy the daily grind of a nine-to-five.

For this reason, there must be an effort to build healthy relationships, or life in the workplace can become untenable for everyone, and productivity will decline.

Leaders need to make their workplace society function positively, with co-operation and respect. In this way everyone is working for the common good and towards a common purpose.

This demands that effective relationships are built upon an understanding of each other's needs. It is no different to how things should be in the home; no personal relationship will last very long if there is a sense that one or both parties are being selfish.

The most effective way to understand how other people are feeling is to listen to what they have to say. This must be done without judging, and not as though you are being forced to do so by some higher authority.

Very often, teams will have the same goals as their leaders, but may just want to know that they are not seen as automatons that have no creative input.

Quality workplace relationships make people feel happy. One of the major reasons why employees move on from a company is because of relationship clashes with leaders or other colleagues.

Leaders should also make sure that they create the circumstances for understanding within their team, and this means asking questions. Assuming that your team will simply pipe up and express their feelings is not enough; many people will not feel it is their place to speak up unless they are specifically asked to do so.

Listening should be done attentively, not glancing at your watch every couple of minutes or trying not to look bored. This means you listen without interrupting or fidgeting, and with the correct expression. Your expression, by the way, should be genuine or you will be found out very quickly and the situation will become worse than had you not asked in the first place.

A great way to foster healthy relationships with your team is by meeting them in a more social environment on regular occasions. Some companies choose to send their staff to regular golfing outings while others prefer to host a monthly BBQ or weekend trips.

Regardless what you end up choosing, the key lies in giving your team a chance to connect away from the daily grind.

Building effective relationships means that neither party must make any assumptions. As a leader, you cannot expect people to understand exactly what we want and why you want it. Sometimes it is this lack of comprehension that causes problems. As much as you must trust your team members to have intelligence, if they are not party to the goals you are working towards they can become resistant.

As far as possible, your team should be conversant with your goals and how their actions are contributing to their successful outcome. Humans are inquisitive and function better when not kept in the dark.

Respect is the key ingredient of any good relationship, and this means respect for yourself as well as others. Genuinely listening and understanding are the ways in which you show that you respect the person you are talking to.

Quickly judging based on preconceived ideas or prejudice is the opposite of having respect. Bear in mind that not everyone will respond in 100% perfect fashion to all that occurs in the workplace.

Although it is not the leader's job to be a permanent shoulder to cry on, it is important to accept that your team is made up of individuals whose lives may not be as perfect as their coffee-break banter might lead you to believe.

Whilst creating a healthy working relationship is a crucial goal, the smart leader will always bear in mind that conflict is inevitable and must be managed, rather than ignored for the sake of apparent peace.

Relationships can never improve unless problems are identified and confronted. Differences between people are inevitable, and hearing them aired can lead to some very useful resolutions that produce ideas beyond the expected.

The alternative is highly detrimental: to let problems fester and build, and ruin the atmosphere in a workplace, if not productivity levels.

Keys for success in working relationships:

1. One party at least should value the relationship – This may start off as a one-way street, but this can lead to a meeting of minds later on.

2. Listen effectively, without judging – Listening in this way will promote mutual understanding and mutual respect.

3. Have informal chats – Chatting over a coffee can encourage a more frank exchange of views than meeting officially with a desk between you.

4. Create an open culture – Your team should know they can speak freely, no matter if that is to express happiness, joy, contentment, anger, irritation, sadness or fear. Negative feelings that are hoarded cause significant problems.

Leaders must take responsibility for their team's performance, which means leaders must be happy that the direction of their team is one which the leader thinks is best.

Although it is useful to have creative sessions with team members to bat around a few ideas, the overarching goals that the team must fulfill are most often set by the leader, or some authority above the leader.

The challenge is therefore to get the team "onside" with the given aims, even when some team members may wholeheartedly disagree with them, or baulk at the idea that these have been imposed on them from above.

Despite the accepted hierarchy of any workplace, for a team to work most efficiently, its members – especially higher level ones – may want to feel they are contributing more than the spade work; they may like to feel that they have chosen where some of the plots should be dug.

This presents a challenge for the leader who cannot just let his or her subordinates have free play. The team must be made to feel involved and motivated. Or perhaps the situation is worse, and your team is beginning to show a little disobedience. How then to provoke a positive response in them?

The answer is by empowering your team, as far as possible. Short of handing over the reins and heading off home, the motivational leader must be able to create a sense that their team is actively involved in the process and contributing in a real sense to the overall outcome of the project.

This can involve learning how to make your suggestions appeal to them. This may mean you solicit their opinions and take the best ideas on board. Or you may have to convince them that your goals are shared and that their futures are tied to your overall success. It may be a simple matter of making an employee understand that their job will be safer if they perform well; reminding them that they are working for themselves and their family, and not just for a company.

However, empowering others does not just mean employing tactics that persuade other people to your own opinion or goals. It can also mean demonstrating leadership qualities that inspire others to act at their very best, no matter what is asked of them. Such leadership qualities would be most in evidence in the armed services, where the end result of potentially being killed is rarely going to elicit a whoop and a cheer. Soldiers are empowered to greatness by the examples set by their commanding officers.

Sometimes, it is just a matter of being an admirable and inspirational human being. Of course, some are born with more of these qualities than others, but we can all strive to lead by example, so that others will feel empowered to make great things happen.

Getting the Most from Your Team

Start right

When a staff member joins your team, give them time to become fully acclimatized to your company. The sooner they settle, the sooner you can start to reap rewards. It will help if you complete an induction and a detailed contract of employment, which outlines what you expect from them.

Create expectations

Strange as it may sound, some employees do not have a clear sense of their role. Such confusion can cause arguments, or even duplication or omission of tasks. This is clearly bad for productivity. Your team needs to know their job and responsibilities; a job description will help.

Stand back

Part of empowering your team is trusting they can get on with the job without you peering over their shoulder every fifteen minutes. If you want staff members to flourish, they should be allowed to get on with their job. Of course you need to keep a watchful eye, but there is a happy medium where they know you trust them. Your team is more likely to over-perform if they feel good about what they are doing. Motivated staff works harder.

Money is often not the prime motivator. They want to know what is expected of them, and then they want to be allowed to get on with it. This is far easier if the right people are employed in the first place.

Communication

Effective communication is the lifeblood of any organization, regardless of its size. That may mean face-to-face talks or pinning notes on a board.

Provided your team knows what's going on, you are being an effective leader. Try asking your team how they prefer communication to happen. This helps to empower them.

Keep communicating

It can happen that there is a sincere intention to improve communication, and it all starts off positively: team briefs, newsletters; intranets, etc. Then things start to slow down. As a leader you should not let this happen. It may mean important information is not imparted, or you are viewed as not bothered how the team is getting on.

Be honest

Communication is not much use if your team believes it is not getting the whole picture. Bad news is still news, and you must trust that your people are mature enough to handle it, or you may find they are insulted and no longer believe what you tell them. This does not mean shouting every piece of office gossip from the rooftop, but it does mean keeping your team abreast of all that is pertinent to them.

Consultation

Effective consultation is a vital tool to improving performance. Your team members have specific roles. Your collective overview may be more knowledgeable, but there may be team members whose specific knowledge is greater than yours.

Asking for their opinion is not weak; it is sensible, and it serves to empower that team member. The more facts you have the easier and more effective your decision-making will be. Getting the most out of your team is greatly aided by effective consultation and it demonstrates respect from you to them.

Training

Training is a boon if it is relevant to the team members receiving it. You are guaranteed to alienate staff by sending them on courses that bear no relevance to their role.

Training for the sake of training is counter-productive. You need to ask: Will the training help the business? Is it geared to the priorities of the business? Are the right individuals and teams within your organization receiving the training? How can I quantify any improvement?

Training must be organized and delivered effectively or you should not commit to it in the first place. Ensure that the agreed priorities are met. Once this happens, think how you can help individual team members in their personal development. This can be a real aid towards improving performance and motivation.

When the training is over, try and evaluate its worth. Where do you expect to see improvements? If you evaluate effectively, you can judge where further investment in training will pay off.

Organizations of all sizes invest in their people through effective training. Your team is your most valuable asset and their performance has an impact on the company's bottom line.

All companies should review performance of their staff on a regular basis. When staff appraisals do not work, it is for the following reasons: There is no system in place for undertaking reviews on a regular basis; there is no paper trail to follow so people don't know where to start; they are used purely to air grievances so become a negative thing; the appraiser isn't trained to appraise so the results are unreliable; there is no follow-up so improvements are missed.

Chapter 7- How to be A Great Business Leader

1. Ask to be judged

Finding out what others think of your leadership skills can really help you change for the better. Sometimes leaders can be so wrapped up in appraising others, that they do not seek appraisal from below, only from their own superiors.

Your team is the best source of feedback, because they are on the receiving end of your "skills" every day. Honesty should be encouraged, but bear in mind that it may only be anonymous feedback that holds the truth if your team believes you are going to use it against them, or become defensive about what they say. If you have created a trusting and open environment, this should not be a problem.

2. Don't abuse your power

If people are questioning why certain things are done, or the logic of decisions, never pull rank in response. Your team should feel empowered, if only by you taking the time to explain the rationale for any decisions that have been made.

Your team must be on your side. This will not happen by you telling them that the decision is the right one because you are the boss. Your team may not agree, but they should know why a situation is how it is.

3. Your team is intelligent and can be trusted

Your team should be allowed to take actions and make decisions. Trust is a vital component of leadership skills. If you can't trust people to do their jobs, then you have the wrong people, or you're not managing them properly.

Let them do what they are there to do without peering over their shoulders every fifteen minutes, asking what they are doing with their time.

4. Listen

Truly listening to your team is one of the greatest leadership skills. Good listeners come across as genuinely interested, empathetic, and concerned to find out what's going on.

All great leaders have great communication skills. Unhappy team members can only exist where their problems have not been aired. Create an environment where problems can be discussed so that solutions can be found.

5. Stop being an expert on everything

Leaders often achieve their positions by being proficient in a certain area, and thus will have an opinion on how to fix problems. They believe it's better to tell someone what to do, or even to do it themselves, than give their team the opportunity to develop their own solutions, and therefore exercise their creativity.

6. Be constructive

Negativity breeds negativity. How you communicate has a profound effect on your team, as a whole and individually. Criticisms will always need to be made by leaders, but try to make them constructive, and deliver them without emotional attachment.

7. Judge your success by your team's

The true success of a leader can be measured by the success of the people who work for them. You cannot be a successful leader of a failing team, just as you cannot be a successful general of a defeated army. Your focus should always be on building your team's skills and removing obstacles in their way.

8. Don't be a narcissist

Nothing is more annoying for team members than leaders who make their decisions based on how good it will make them appear to their superiors. A key leadership skill is integrity. Integrity is about doing the right thing, and allowing praise where praise is due, even if that is not at your door.

9. Have a sense of humor

People work better when they are enjoying themselves. The work itself may be dull, but the environment does not have to be. Stifling fun also means stifling creativity. Team members love it when the leader joins in and has fun. This does not have to create a flippant atmosphere; on the contrary, this is a tenet of team-building.

10. Don't be too distant

Without revealing you innermost secrets, it is possible for leaders to show a more human side. If mutual respect exists, this should not be seen as vulnerability, rather a sign that you are a sentient human being, just as your team members are.

Only when your team gets to know the real you will the true foundations of good leadership be properly established – trust and respect.

Sun Tzu, writing in the 5th century BC in The Art of War said: "What enables the wise sovereign and the good general to strike and conquer and achieve things beyond the reach of ordinary men is foreknowledge."

This is an as-yet-unmentioned attribute of a great leader – the ability to predict. No matter how many managerial and people skills the business leader possesses, they will all be jeopardized if he or she cannot anticipate the effects of the plans they put in place, and the actions they take. In this respect, it may be that their age and experience must take precedence over consultation with the "troops", who may little understand the ramifications of what is about to take place.

This is where the genuine leader comes to the fore and truly claims their title. When all around are scratching their heads and reluctant to make a decision, old-style leadership must come into play. The modern leader may utterly fail in this scenario for lack of guts and an over-familiarity with their team.

As Sun Tzu says: "Some leaders are generous but cannot use their men. They love their men but cannot command them… These leaders create spoiled children. Their soldiers are useless."

Leadership may have become a different beast over the years, but it is still, at its heart, about leading.

ABOUT THE AUTHOR

Rafael Johnson is a very ambitious man. He was born and raised in Delaware, but he always dreams big. He wants to be known and be acknowledged in his field of expertise. As early as thirteen years old, he was determined to own a ship yard and not just work in a ship yard.

True enough, he studied hard and stayed focus. Now, he wants to inspire others and help them to achieve their dreams in the process; that is why he wrote this book.